Urban Temple
sijo, twisted & straight

Urban Temple
sijo, twisted & straight

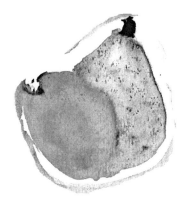

David McCann

BO-LEAF

 BO-LEAF

Published by Bo-Leaf Books
www.boleafbooks.com

First printing
10 9 8 7 6 5 4 3 2 1

Book design by Bo-Leaf Studio.

"Locomotive" first appeared in *Kaimana,* special double issue,
2002-2006. An earlier version of "Over the Edge" appeared in
Epoch, vol. 57, no. 3.

ISBN 978-0-9768086-3-3

For Richard McCann

INTRODUCTION

I have been reading, translating and listening to performances of sijo for over thirty years. I wrote my first sijo in Korean years ago, about an evening in the town of Andong when I had come back from a late night of drinking *makkŏlli*, singing, telling stories, and reciting poems. Some time after that, I was struck by a newspaper column that Yi Pyŏnggi wrote "On Revitalization of the Sijo" calling for new language, ideas, images and gestures in the sijo—especially, writing sijo to be *read*—that might make it live again in the modern world.

With these and other ideas in mind, small wonder that I finally started writing sijo in English. Prompted by the sight of the two lobster tanks standing by the entrance to my favorite restaurant, I took out my pen, grabbed a napkin, and started with "All through lunch, from my table/I keep an eye on your disputes,/green lobsters in the bubbling/tank by the restaurant door." The sense of confinement; the desire to break free: I must have been feeling like a lobster in my own tank.

As I wrote the poems in this collection, I felt like an explorer. My writing tends to happen in certain places: at home, or up in Maine at the family cottage, in Seoul and elsewhere in Korea, whenever I am stirred by feeling, by something observed. From that moment in the fall of 2006, all of my poetry writing has been in the sijo form in English.

The sijo is a vernacular Korean verse form. While there are many variants, the standard form, known as the *p'yŏng sijo*, has three lines, each having four segments. The first two lines of the sijo present and develop the topic, while the third line introduces a "twist," a new turn, direction, or term, then moves through a slightly expanded second segment to the conclusion.

The sijo form compresses the rhetorical features of the Classical Chinese quatrain—presentation, development, then a twist, and a conclusion or resolution—into three lines. Each sijo line tends to be in two parts, with each part in turn being a two-part phrase or clause; thus there are four parts per sijo line. Syllable count is a significant feature of the sijo—3 4 3 4 (or 3 4 4 4) syllables for lines one and two, and then 3 5 4 3 in the final line. Most of the sijo in this collection follow this pattern, although some variations occur, as is the case in Korean practice now and in the past. Greater regularity in syllable count is found where the line and sense of the poem need to stabilize themselves in order to make a shift, either from line to line, or through the rhetorical twist that starts the third line.

A big twist happened to the sijo in the 20th century, as professional, modern poets confronted the change from sijo told or sung (or both) in performance, to the enterprise, instead, of writing sijo poems that were to be printed, published, purchased, and read. Yi Pyŏnggi's efforts to revitalize sijo practice, to turn it into a form that could be appreciated by contemporary readers, impelled his own sijo toward the understated specifics of modern life, as in his gently beautiful "Orchid":

> In one hand holding a book
>   drowsing away, then suddenly awake:
> the bright sun arcs overhead,
>   a cool wind rises, while
> the orchid, two or three buds,
>   has opened up, full and wide.*

Many of the elements of Yi's sijo had their counterparts in traditional sijo practice. The phrase "in one hand" appears in several earlier sijo, as do alternating states of drowsing and waking. The poem has the familiar feel of an old story. What gives it a modern flavor, though, and locates the poem, the writer and the reader in the present day, is the reference to the product of the new publishing houses—the "book"— sold in the new stores in the new commercial districts of Seoul to readers who might take it home and—Who knows?—find themselves, like the orchid and the narrator, awakened too.

David McCann
Watertown, 2010

---

* See *AZALEA: Journal of Korean Literature & Culture*, Volume Two, Korea Institute, Harvard University 2008, p. 368, for a slightly different version.

CONTENTS

Part Two
Vast, the C

Part Three
Tag & Release

Part One

Urban Temple

Urban Temple

Early morning bell rings its

3

and someone begins chanting the sutras.

Dok Dok Dok Dok

he beats the wood.

Eyes half closed half open,
the Buddha sits smiling.

Belief practice practice belief.

First Sijo: A Night in Andong

One night in Andong
   after a tour of back-alley wine shops,

head spinning, I staggered down
   the narrow, paddy-field paths,

when the two pigs grunted grunted
   "So, you! Home at last?"

하룻밤 안동시내 골목술집 구경하고

머리가 삥삥돌때 밭둑길을 거닐다가

도야지 꿀꿀 소리야 이제왔노 하노라

Where King Munmu Ordered His Ashes Scattered

Among the stars
that lie scattered
days when hardly a sound

above the waters
where a king's remains remain

gulls wheel and bank.

Two youngsters facing out,
one then the other
skipping stones out to the king's tomb,

while far to the northeast, seven missiles fall into a
    circle in the water.

Paekdam Temple

Incense-full, replete with books,
    scrolls, photographs, documents
memorializing Manhae,
    Ten Thousand Seas, Korea icon.
He'd have laughed, how Paekdam Temple
    at Mount Sŏrak makes him such space.

Lone Island

The sea below filled with boats,
    Ulleung Island watching them work.
Soon we will fly over Dokdo, Lone Island,
    in Japanese, *Takeshima.*
Cut the crap! Territorial disputes
    at thirty-thousand feet appear pointless.

That tiny thing is Dokdo?
    It must be a boat instead.
But a boat without a wake?
    A hundred times the size of other boats?
No wonder! Lone Island got that name
    for a reason. Leave it alone!

Where the Declaration
Was Printed In a Night

This park,
I see it now the sign says it plain:

Here the press stood that printed
35 thousand copies
of the Korean Independence Declaration.

Stayed up all night to do it too, the staff,
their other halves
muttering warnings.

Ah my love this land
this small park will

be forever remembered as we
read the words and lift the pages up,
the whole people carry them out into the streets.

We reach out to steady ourselves
against the wall, we are getting older every minute,
this land, my love, Ah this small park!

Landscape Calligraphy

In the old days never
an issue,

Korea men simply pissed where they wished

on a wall up an alley
or by the side of the road

Moonlit or Grand Style,
intermittent or steady

brushstrokes redefining
the country or urban scene,

perspective modestly shifting its gaze
as they finished the job of letting it
go where it wished.

Korea's Strangely First

This small shop
where a woman sits making custom dresses

the house where Yi Sang lived,

post before anyone else knew *modern.*

Seoul, 2006, June

No sign of
the small stray cat,

two days now
since it emerged,
unkempt kitten barely
able to wobble
out from under the bush.

The plastic cup
today holds nothing but rain.

Hush Now, Hush

Royal park, the famous old bridge
    where a man and woman stand facing.
They cannot cross, the bridge would fall;
    cannot part, this world and the next.
He cries out, *Mother!* She stills him
    with a gesture, and vanishes.

Pottery Kiln in Kyŏngju

We should do this every day!

Earth water hand wheel fire.

There is no perfection in the firing,
only what will be found will be found.

Water soaked leather band better to shape the thrown.

Strips wood slat knives,

two thousand years spanking the clay.

Earth from a field
wood from the forest

intent

what takes shape in the interplay.

Locomotive

Seoul-Pusan Line

Crazy reason you
draw me fast
through your country.

One tree bends under
the weight of another and another and another
very fat magpie.

A single leaf lets go,
Nude
descending my stare,

while outside the windows
landscape strips itself naked in its race to stay
right where it was.

Reading Jeffers on the Flight Home

How hawk light shifts across
porous wedges of wooded headland
lowering into the waves
as they keep it up, steady recitation,

first whispers then shouts slamming themselves
at the rockface.

A gull screeches across this slim expanse.
Everything it sees makes it yell.

Higgins Beach, August, 2006

How thin it seems, the night sky,
always presenting itself.

Big Dipper, Little, None,
The Sieve, all that extravagant display
of empty night sky.

This morning taking down beach towels
from the line out back, I look
out over the neighbor's yard
through the gap where last night the North Star
danced between the trees.

House at the Center of the Universe

See how the clouds now do their work
against all odds, nature stacked against it,
an onshore breeze and still they make
their way out over the water.

A monarch keeps circling,
or does the house sit on some butterfly path?
Another flutters by, delicately battling the breeze.

An arc of birds veers past,
above the reach of one fisherman advancing cautiously
into the waves.

Oceanic Cold

Wireless predictability
of all these chances the most likely,
how the stream's flow appears uniform,
obscures back-pulls.

From the vantage point of sufficient distance or time
it seems human, the long slow process of growing old
as it vanishes to a flicker,

one among thousands of brilliant faceted flashes
from the waves' faces, where moonlight's broad
redeeming gesture breaks apart into recombinatory
incandescence, one might say if it were not
all so unfathomably cold.

Wave Theory

Apart from the birds
just two solitaries
this foggy morning.

Wait wait!
The little one turns and runs
from one parent to the other,
back up the beach.

Wave jumpers
become a woman left standing,
her small white dog
glimmering in the haze.

Watching Birds

arrange themselves in tear-shaped groups on
    the sand

nestled in, or standing one-legged, heads
    turned, beaks tucked

into soft feathers at the base of the necks

while another group crowding along the ridge
    line spills down where the roof reaches,

watching as the weather rises, time to time
    shifting points of balance

till one leaps or falls and flies off

until at last all rise into the air at once,
    pirouetting, screeching out the hymn

in their fearsome voices at the soul that soars
    across the water

Part Two

Vast, the C

Like a martini: three lines with a twist

All through lunch, from my table
    I keep an eye on your disputes,
green lobsters in the bubbling
    tank by the restaurant door.
Slights, fights, bites—Whatever the cause,
    make peace and flee, escape with me!

The feeder hangs suspended
    outside the glass of the window.
On the couch, I sit watching doves,
    swarms of sparrows, chickadees in pairs.
All the mess and noisy disputation
    two cardinals end with *Let there be red!*

The Realm of Birds

Ingratiating dimwit, sparrow
    on the garden path
darts and spins, grins,
    looking back past its shoulder.
Squawk he may, there's no bush to hide
    from the raptor's chilly eye.

A crabshell overturned, dorsal
    side up, with an inch-wide hole
smashed into the center,
    legs and insides all gone,
a sure sign some roving gull
    has fed again and flown on.

Found (NewEnglandMoves.com)

Located in Brookline's
Fisher Hill, this stately
1890 Colonial
residence welcomes all
who enter through its gracious reception
hall with warm oak woods.

Lost

Warm oak woods
    too deep for us to penetrate,
we linger instead
    in the graceful periphery,
while a dog chases hopelessly after
    wooden balls struck so well the mallets sing.

Speed Limit

Into the light the way cars
move on their own beams'
discoveries, meddlesome
yet with an air of inevitability,
we walk on, close to the speed limit
of 65 and getting closer each day.

There are days we seem surrounded
by a cold fog, others when the sun
is flat-out too hot to endure.
This morning, though, as I stopped
on my way from shower to dressing,
where you lay on the bed reading,

I had the story of last night's dream
to tell, of a kitten, bright colored
orange, black, and white, that found us
at some complicated picnic.
A good omen, we agreed, while somewhat
distracted by my nakedness.

Metaphor

What they wrote about gardens
    the rocks, flowers, birds, butterflies:
metaphor, dis-simile,
    a way to write away from this:
she was ink to his darting brush,
    their story grew down the white sheet.

Late Night Reading

No detective story, no crime.
    Just a bunch of situations.
I return to bed. The cat
    has gone into another room.
Somehow my fingers manage to
    wrap themselves into hers.

Tree to the Wind

Come, I want you in me
    wind, whispered the tree.
Fill my branches and leaves,
    weave around my trunk.
Let your sighs become moan when you
    set breath to the opening beneath my heart.

Third Line

O braid me a lightweight, three-ply
   hempen rope, that I may climb!

Leverage

How to shift the weight of waves
    from the land back to surges;
what lever to lift the fog that lies
    heavy still on the horizon;
up the steps to the cottage porch,
    someone tries to calculate.

Dirty white, gulls flying past,
    Don't be so fixed upon refuse!
Search the cliffs for Scholar Stones,
    the sand for gleaming shells.
But the winds carry my scavengers
    past fallacy to the point.

How open the days littered
    with brilliant mornings beckoning,
and still the waters splaying
    their sleek fingers at the shore;
how live it, the span of days, months,
    or even years, to the end.

Too hot, this! The day, the air,
    the sun that flattens wills beneath it.
A lobster boat works its way
    buoy to buoy, pauses off the rocks.
Starboard side, metal crane and pulley
    raise the streaming trap, the green prey.

Last Call

In memory of Ike, Yi Ik-hun

We've all gathered, small banquet room,
    the Lotte Hotel downstairs;
idle chatter, or meeting,
    first-time greetings, kidding around.
Until now, when our patient host
    carefully steps, takes his place.

His face is full, his hair's grown back;
    expression, sharp apprehension.
He takes command as usual,
    but sharper tongued, more to the point.
"Tell me now if you need a guide
    or not. Decide. Up to you."

All the Rest

For Marshall Pihl

Down from the valleys, luminous clouds
    brought their light rains to greet us.
You would call from the balcony
    as they draped the Buddhist temple,
"Look at this," or just as likely,
    "What are you up to in there?"

Winter gown, white monochrome,
    gives way to dirt down payment.
All the rest of your life now lies before us,
    who never imagined
how much whirled in the air around your head
    when you laughed, where you walked.

Over the Edge

If ever I had a sense
    of who I was and where I was
going, how to get there any
    better, clearer than the water
pouring down over the rocks, deep
    into the inviting chasm

bisecting space, creating
    the occasion for this bridge
I stand on looking out to-
    ward the lake, the hills west, the sun
beginning to fall along its
    suggestive, slow arc, the easing

down into the dark, rocks barely
    discernible, in the morning
the first to walk down the path through
    the gorge might say, What, what is that,
there in the water, the lower
    part of the pool? Something. Caught.

The Common Leaf

Fallen leaves, silver and red,
    even black, heavy with rain,
scattered here or mostly there
    for anyone to pick up and use
to shoot down a basketball player,
    a third-grade boy, a young girl.

But someone makes these leaves,
    complicated systems of veins
that feed them, branch-born display
    for sightseers or buyer's gaze.
Want a leaf? You can pick one up
    on the corner. Just bring cash.

The trio cruising the streets
    in the car they've just stolen
(important part of the ritual)
    turn the corner, say "Next one's it."
Three climbs out and shoots the kid where he stands,
    using nothing but a leaf.

Common as leaves in the fall streets,
    neighborhood yards, the school playground;
the passing winds may pick them up
    and whirl them against the fence.
No harm meant, by a leaf. Can't blame
    a leaf for what the wind does.

Rage

All my life, or just this far,
    I've lived fearful of such outbursts
as broke the stern silences
    of carefully built interchange.
What I meant! The pitiful dream of days
    so still no harm was ever done.

The governor's transfer of funds,
    to say nothing of its purpose,
is read by some as a cry
    for help, bail-out, tough position.
Twenty-two, the one who beat, burned, and pissed
    his girlfriend's son—a monster!

The governor's no monster,
    whatever else he may well be.
Quite undone by the pressures
    of office, his fear of Heights;
bought a girl, used her for an hour,
    hoping, or not, to get caught.

Flung a book down on the floor
    right by the cat, I was so mad
at what he'd done, the mess; broken
    sand dollar from the beach in Maine.
Flung down, mess, and most of all, *so mad:*
    I try but can't grasp such rage.

He beat the child with a belt
        until the blood stained the floor.
He burned the child's genitals
        with a cigarette, and then
where he sat in the warm water
        of the bath tub, pissed his head.

Violent, predatory,
        given to bursts of pure rage,
specimens such as I am
        should be locked up, just put away.
Let me sit alone in the dark
        forever. Out? When I'm dead.

Beach Generator

Sun struck waves bearing surfers
    in their black suits, repetitive;
the long line of barnacled
    seaweed and gull clad rocks intervenes;
electric, the waves' toss, hits and rests,
    moves through pools, alternating, direct.

Watch the gull, it knows a thing
    or two about waves, they bear
good things to shore, overturn the dead,
    preparation for a bolted meal;
or landward, the halting elderly man
    waving his arms is tossing bread.

Richmond Island

Looking out, where the bay, bright,
    pulses slowly in the afternoon sun:
Richmond Island, its rocky shore
    on one side, horizon line:
A white gull makes its steady way
    searching, scanning land, waves, for food.

At the beach, tides rise, birds soar,
    the sands lie smooth and wet
or dry, rippled, Edwardian collar
    along the upper edge, below the road.
Eight surfboards with their dark-suited riders
    rest in a line, perfectly still.

Vast, the C

Vast, the C that starts the word
    Crustacean, closed on one side,
open to all the alphabet
    of possibilities out the other.
Crabs, lobsters, a great pile of shrimp:
    Let the feast begin, shells cracking!

From Richmond across to Wood,
    along the sharp line of the horizon,
not a boat, a single gull,
    nor more than the smallest waves.
But just look! There, the flash of sun
    as a boat turns and heads back out.

With the glasses I count twenty-two boats:
    lobstermen out in the bay,
a line of sails hull down
    at the horizon.
Closer in, the row of surfers still
    maintaining their innocence.

B. S. O.

James Levine, Seiji O.
    The B.S.O. Bobby Karol,
Viola, in the photo
    forty years past, sits, head turned.
He taught me guitar, though one morning
    the lesson was his listening.

The usual tale of mixed-up
    communications, parents, children.
My girlfriend's father had composed
    a one-act opera of slurs
he told her I'd been performing.
    Decompose that? Just practice!

Sins, Virtues

In traffic, every driver
    has precedence, the right to merge.
All-way stop, an occasion
    to wave other drivers through.
But horn blasts from behind are not kind.
    Boston drivers, the rush home?

All the same, the effect's cause,
    what science says its object is.
The night sky reflected, waves
    of moonlight, flying carpet.
Left for days, a pair of old shoes
    on the top step, the cottage porch.

Avarice, the root of all
    humans suffer; alphabetic
first among the deadly sins.
    Confucius said, Thought Not Greed.
Buddha taught, All suffering begins with desire.
    Extinguish that? Nirvana!

Emotive, assuredly not
    parallel nor distinctive
universe I occupy
    simultaneously intending
to dwindle away to nothing,
    flock of sparrows at the feeder.

Too Ill to Talk

That last day, too ill to talk
    after the chat with my father,
I said I'd call next morning
    and catch up some with mother.
Telephone: its ringing brought the news.
    We are alone. She is gone.

September one year ago,
    vacation done, the beach visit,
a last trip to Korea.
    Who could have known October's blight?
We are left to endure the silent treatment,
    and she is gone, still, always.

Winning is overrated,
    vastly. Losing is everything.
Losing weight, or altitude,
    bringing it back where it began.
My mother lay down on the floor
    one day last year. We are lost.

Monadnock

Not so much a problem of time
    as instead a way to dispute
how the trees seek to extend
    dominion over us all.
If I said the air is perfectly
    still, then would you believe me?

Paddling out, straining to turn
    round to see Monadnock,
halfway across Gilmore Pond
    and still no sign of the Mount.
Sudden gust of wind spins the kayak,
    and there it is, bare stone topped!

Part Three

Tag & Release

What I Want

Avarice, envy denied,
    frustrated, sublimated.
What I want I need and deserve;
    I need to have what you possess,
Your calm skill as you swim the lake
    to the float where I lie gasping.

Your Hands

Your hands held nothing but heartbreak as you smiled
and extended them to me.

Your eyes wished away sadness when you spoke and
turned to leave.

Only dreams bring such songs as never you sang in
your life or mine.

Onset

The twin oak back by the house
    has been drilled, carved deep for grubs.
The woodpeckers heard them chewing,
    worked their intricate necklace of pits.
"This one's dead!" Bill shouts in anger,
    whacking the trunk with his cane.

Of All Such Signs

About to get ridiculous,
    petals furled pink flags of spring
will let shout on every block
    the joyous noise of profusion.
Still as death, memories unwind
    of my young friend, this season.

Of all such signs the most tendentious,
    how we would agree and yet disdain
the truth found by reduction, proof,
    the only way out ever found.
Martinis, you said, that last night
    in Seattle, are just gin.

That obese man waddling past
    the row of seats by the gate, just now,
has by the sign of face, jowls, chin, cheeks,
    outlived you by ten years, I'd guess.
Out of shape, however defined,
    still, his gaze is forward, home.

"Shaman Frogs"

Manhae Village, Mt. Sŏrak

It's raining, frogs suddenly
    break out in song, the forest still.
Raining still, and the frogs, stilled
    for a round, break out in song.
The forest, all its green sound hushed
    by the night rain, the dark night.

At Manhae Village

Mystified by the dark light
    yet eager to try the drum,
the great bell, hollow wood fish,
    bronze hammered plaque that calls the birds,
one by one, as the monk calls us
    we step forward and begin.

Midang's House

At the end there is nothing.
    Metal gate, hinges broken.
At the end there was hunger.
    Someone hired cooked meals and cleaned.
At the end, just the two of them;
    outside the gate, the old pine.

Park by Chogye Temple, Seoul, 2008

Little cat, Dear Mother,
    three friends who have passed away.
Head bowed, I sit on a bench
    in the small park and pray.
Bamboo leaves in the passing wind
    whisper, at peace; and I am.

Wobbly kitten, how you've grown!
    Two years old, orange and white,
resident queen of that small park,
    you crouched on the slope and watched
me bend down in happy disbelief
    as we meet again in this way.

Into Your Traces

Such silence as now surrounds
    this very place where you once lived,
fallen leaves stirred by winds,
    then laid flat by sheets of rain;
not mellow, fruitfulness, resigned
    acceptance. No. The streets heave

up from the harbor, crossing
    bridges roaring, traffic heavy,
turning east, bending always
    to the sun's rise where light begins
to find us, intent, silhouettes
    leaning down into your traces.

Early Summer

They say the trees this time of year
    are mostly still, by which they mean
the winds don't move them much, the limbs
    stir but slightly, leaves not at all.
This strange peace! Only the squirrel
    knows no difference, never stops.

I said I'd never let it
    get this deep or personal.
I said take this glass arm
    and stick it, that he might fly.
Bell buoy, half a mile out and riding;
    waves big as houses crash on shore.

Wedding Picture, with Crows

Returning, I walked past a flock
    of fifty crows busily engaged
flipping fallen leaves, hop hop,
    plip plip, then beaking the dirt.
Wedding group, bride in white, attendants'
    satin dresses, tuxedoes.

In a language strange to me
    the photographer and crew
set themselves, the wedding party,
    around a tree they climbed to shoot
as I walked under my umbrella
    on through the sound of the rain.

One for Ann

Like a squirrel digging nuts up
    or those crows turning dead leaves
over, I go places and take
    poems, this one from the back seat
of the cab on its way to the airport.
    When I get home, it's all yours.

My Father Writing Sijo

My father now at ninety-two
    has started writing sijo.
The first seemed operatic:
    two voices, alto and bass.
My mother's earnest questioning,
    his aria, "Never More."

Wave

Sun is up, the surf quiet.
> A wave, and soon enough, another.

Couples strolling, silhouetted;
> a lobster boat's white transom, west.

I hear these: each wave in sequence,
> granddaughter's laugh as she wakes.

Prouts Neck

Private is as private does:
    enterprise, a bathroom.
This less than half-mile run
    of asphalt road along the coast:
They own it, the homes that line it.
    All *Property*, and *Private*.

Steeps

Often the tea leaf opened
on a chilly hillside under the sun
steeps in a pot that is in generic terms the tea steeps

Often enough I wish the stones had fallen earlier
when I was a child visiting that beach in Maine
turning dark in the sun running in the shallows

splash splash that child steeped in the tide pool
draining the entire visible expanse of beach, sand wide,
into the glistening aluminum water

The Old Motel

Drove two hours north of Portland
    and east, some, turned south
down the point toward Pemaquid.
    Road, cars, *Antiques*, *Italian Sandwiches*.
Glimpsed at last, *Motel Cottages*.
    A brief landing, then down the path.

Gravel drive gives way to grass
    speckled with small yellow flowers.
A swing, rope tied round and round
    the limb broken off, eight inches thick.
Arrive here, at the wooden dock:
    the cove's wide reach, dark water.

The flow is upstream with the tide.
    Minnows flicker in schools and veer.
Tributary, recipient:
    the long calming intake of breath.
An osprey crosses overhead;
    a flock of ducks splashes down.

Surfing in Maine

Today's forecast calls for a line
        of agile optimists
sitting just off the coast in dark suits
        rising periodically to
nature's call. They yearn for sets of five:
        tag and release, rise and ride.

Family Beach Cottage

What I don't know about trusts
    and estates would fill a book
on the subject, a lawyer's head,
    an office's special practice.
Take this house, for example, please.
    Teach me to keep, or let go.

Milky Way Railroad

We all seem to be taking
    something. Pills, water, vacation.
Last night outside the cottage
    calling you on the cellphone,
overhead the starry night sky,
    the Milky Way took my breath.

A train whistle, but here at the beach?
    Driving up yesterday
with my father, we crossed a rise
    just as a train rattled beneath.
Railroad bridge I'd never noticed.
    Chance encounter, altered ear.

Real Estate

On this walk so far I think
    I have gathered dozens of them:
Sand dollars, large, small, bright, dull,
    even orange, strange currency.
Down payment! Sand castle, dripped walls
    and turrets, moat; these poems.

Away

Memories—Do they go out
    like the tides, or a light?
Diminish like a bank account?
    Or like a pair of socks, just shrink?
Labor Day. Faculty friends would ask,
    So, where did you go last summer?

One sure thing: If I don't write
    every morning, I don't write at all.
There's something about the light, air,
    the way traffic has gone on its way.
Cardinal just now at the feeder
    speaks in a language of scattered clicks.

Just "Away," autoreply
    to all e-mail, including mine.
What a joy, deliberately
    to write anything and next moment
read "I'm gone. All e-links are bad here.
    If I can, I'll reply soon."

Notes

Where King Munmu Ordered His Ashes
Scattered   p.19
King Munmu established the Silla Kingdom, reigning
from 661 to 681. He ordered that his ashes be placed
just off the coast east of the Silla capitol of Kyŏngju so
that his dragon spirit could protect the kingdom. On
July 4, 2006, North Korea test-fired a series of missiles
over what is called the East Sea.

Paekdam Temple   p.20
Manhae was the Buddhist name as well as the *nom de
plume* of the monk, poet, and independence leader Han
Yongun, 1879-1944. He entered Buddhist orders at
Paekdam Temple, located in the Sŏrak Mountains near
the east coast of Korea. A memorial museum has been
established there.

Lone Island   p.21
Lone Island, a small rock island off the east coast of
Korea, is also claimed by Japan.

Korea's Strangely First   p. 24
Yi Sang, 1910-1937, was a poet, architect, novelist, and
short story writer.

Hush Now, Hush   p. 26
The setting of the poem, Deoksu Palace is located in
the old center of Seoul, at City Hall Plaza.

At Manhae Village   p. 68

Manhae Village is a new study and practice center where students of all kinds can explore Manhae Han Yongun's writings, the history of his role during the 1919 Independence Movement and after, as well as his poetry. His 1925 collection, *The Silence of Love*, remains a landmark in 20th-century Korean literature.

Midang's House   p. 69

The poet Midang, Sŏ Chŏngju, 1915-2000, one of Korea's great 20th-century poets, was ignored or vilified in his last years for his "pro-Japanese" and "pro-government" opinions. For a period in the late 1980's he and his wife were driven into exile in the United States by threats of physical violence. Their house in the Kwanak section of Seoul has been empty, abandoned since their deaths, within months of each other, at the end of the year 2000. The City of Seoul is now restoring the property and building a memorial.

Afterword

The sijo has a history that goes back centuries in Korea, and the form continues to draw many practitioners today. The sijo's origins are not clear in a formal sense, since the Korean alphabet was invented only in the 15th century, while many sijo are said to predate it. Originally, the sijo was a musical form, part of a tradition of oral story-telling and song performance that was not written down and printed until the 18th century. When sung, the sijo is characterized by long, drawn-out vocal expression—not so much to a given melody as set into an established rhythmic pattern. While sijo can be sung solo, they are often accompanied by the hourglass-shaped drum, the *ch'ang'go*, which is also used with the Korean story-telling narrative form known as *p'ansori*. Sijo vocalization can be powerfully expressive; for accomplished singers, the mastery of volume control, pitch change, and the breath is achieved only with a great deal of study and practice. On the other hand, all of the vocalization patterns are perfectly natural extensions of ordinary speech and calling, so even an amateur can sing a sijo that sounds recognizably like the real thing.

While a great number of Korea's traditional sijo are embedded in historical narratives, others are by or about people who were not part of the ruling *yangban* class. Their works have a sometimes humorous, sometimes poignant tone. There are dozens of sijo said to have been composed by *kisaeng* women, members of an entertainment profession somewhat like the Japanese geisha. The most famous of all was Hwang Chini, author of a half dozen truly remarkable sijo, as well as a number of poems in Classical Chinese. Though two or three of her sijo poems compete for the greatest esteem, I find one most striking, both for its poignant subject, and even more, its technical accomplishment.

어져 내일이야 그릴줄을 모로다냐
이시라 하더면 가랴마난 제 구타여
보내고 그리난 情은 나도 몰라 하노라

Oh no! What have I done?
    I didn't know what it was to yearn!
If I'd said, *You, just stay,*
    could he have gone? But stubborn, I
sent him away, and now what longing
    truly is, I've come to learn.

Notably, in the original, the diction of this poem is almost entirely and purely Korean, with the one exception of the term 情 *chŏng*, (longing) feeling. The vast majority of other sijo poems by Hwang Chini share with the Korean language itself a fairly broad use of Sino-Korean, Chinese-origin terms. Sijo poems from the 16th and 17th centuries seem to have more of a Sino-Korean vocabulary, perhaps reflecting their ruling class origins, while those from the later centuries use less, perhaps in turn reflecting a popularization of the form and practice. But with Hwang Chini's sijo poem, there is no mix, no drift, only the expression of strong, direct feeling pouring forth in nearly pure Korean.

    The poem's other technical accomplishment is its deft use of enjambment, the run-on line, at the end of line two, where the sense of the poem rushes past the usual sentence or clause ending form, through the continuative form *kut'ayŏ,* "deliberately," into the "twist" at the beginning of line three, where the longing and the remaining have already turned irreversibly to "sent him away," *ponaego.*

Sijo histories take note of a shift in the 17th and 18th centuries toward an expanded form known as the *sasŏl,* or "narrative" sijo and many theories and practices were tried out in the first half of the 20th century to make sijo modern. In North Korea, the sijo is denigrated for its historic identity as an upper-class literary pursuit, but such disapproval requires that one overlook the sijo's vernacular Korean linguistic base, a contrast to the literary Chinese expression that was in fact always a marker of ruling class records, communications, and literary works.

In South Korea, the sijo continues to find many practitioners, of all generations. In fact, the journal *Onul ŭi sijo,* or *Sijo Today,* started up just a year ago, and in its recent issue #2 published work by more than seventy poets.

Those who wish to read more about the sijo in Korea are urged to consult Richard Rutt's *The Bamboo Grove,* and the other volumes on the recommended reading list.

Recommended Reading

Richard Rutt, *The Bamboo Grove: An Introduction to Sijo*. The University of Michigan Press, Ann Arbor, 1998.

David R. McCann, *Early Korean Literature, Selections and Introductions*. Columbia University Press, New York, 2000.

Kevin O'Rourke, *The Book of Korean Shijo*. Harvard University Press, Cambridge, 2002.

Peter H. Lee, *The Columbia Anthology of Traditional Korean Poetry*. Columbia University Press, New York, 2002.

David R. McCann, "Korean Literature and Performance? Sijo!" *AZALEA: Journal of Korean Literature & Culture*, Volume Two. Korea Institute, Harvard University, 2008.

Acknowledgments

To *Munhak Sasang* journal, Seoul, my thanks for the October 2008 issue, which featured my sijo poems and project, and to Kwŏn Kyŏng-Mi and the sijo poet Hong Sŏngnan for their translations of "Urban Temple"; "Seoul, June, 2006"; "Landscape Calligraphy"; "Too Ill to Talk"; "Tree to the Wind"; "Deoksu Palace, Seoul"; and "Lone Island." I also thank the poet Lee Keun-bae for his own translation of "Lone Island," published in *Munhak ŭi Munhak*, Fall, 2007.

My thanks to the poets of Every Other Thursday, John Hildebidle, Susan Donnelly, Polly Brown, Sarah Bennett, John Hodgen, Con Squires, Deborah Melone, and Bonnie Bishop, for their encouragement and interest over the past two years as I have explored the sijo form; to Paul Hamill, for his friendship as well as his own forays into the form, and to the poetry translation group O.S.I.P., in Ithaca, especially Gail Holst-Warhaft, for determination to live up to the name Organization for Singing International Poetry; to Mark Taylor, at the Bancroft School, for the invitation to present a sijo workshop to the creative writing club, and to the Bancroft students themselves for their own wonderfully creative work that day. I recall the warm encouragement, years ago, that Professor Chŏng Pyŏnguk of Seoul National University provided me, then a graduate student, when I first began my study of the sijo form and its history; his *Dictionary of Sijo Literature* has been one of my guidebooks for the past three decades. I owe special thanks to Professor Kwon Youngmin of Seoul National University for his friendship and guidance over the years. Anne Dalton, the publisher of Bo-Leaf Books, has been a perceptive and persistent guide on the journey toward this book, and I am delighted to note my gratitude to her, here on this page. To my family—my wife Ann, our daughter Kate and her husband Mark and their daughter Helen, our son Max and his wife Jenn, my loving thanks for being there, inside and outside these poems.

About the Author

David McCann is an award-winning poet, scholar, and translator. His poems have appeared in such distinguished journals as *Poetry, Ploughshares,* and *Prairie Schooner.* His recent collection of poems, *The Way I Wait For You,* was published by Codhill Press in 2007. Winner of a Pushcart Prize for poetry, he has also been the recipient of numerous other prizes, grants, and fellowships including the Korean Cultural Order of Merit (2006), the prestigious Manhae Prize in Arts and Sciences (2004), and the Korea P.E.N. Center Translation Prize (1994).

He is currently the Korea Foundation Professor of Korean Literature in the Department of East Asian Languages and Civilizations as well as Director of the Korea Institute at Harvard University.

Other Works by David McCann

Poetry
The Way I Wait For You. Codhill Press, 2007.
Cat Bird Tree (chapbook). Pudding House, 2005.

Translations
Azaleas: a book of poems (by Kim Sowŏl). Columbia University Press, 2007.
Enough to Say It's Far: Poems by Pak Chaesam (with Jiwon Shin), Princeton University Press, 2006.
Traveler Maps: Poems by Ko Un. Tamal Vista Publications, 2004.

Korean Studies
The Columbia Anthology of Modern Korean Poetry, editor and translator. Columbia University Press, 2004.
Early Korean Literature: Selections and Introductions. Columbia University Press, 2000.
Selected Poems of Sŏ Chŏngju. Columbia University Press, 1989.
Prison Writings of Kim Dae Jung (with Ch'oi Sungil). University of California Press, 1987.

Breinigsville, PA USA
21 June 2010
240227BV00001B/6/P

9 780976 808633